CW00589638

For Rich,

for his constant love, support,
belief & encouragement xx

INTRODUCTION

Any miniaturist or dollshouse enthusiast will know that tiny items rarely have tiny prices, so the key point to this book is that the projects utilise materials that you probaby already have at home, and in fact might even be about to throw away! But if you do need to buy something all the materials are readily and cheaply available.

The projects here are intended for a 12th scale dollshouse, but many are 'made to measure' and so could be adapted for a slightly different size. Each project has full colour, easy to follow, photo instructions and most of the items are fairly simple to make. But I strongly recommend reading through any project right to the end before you start cutting or sticking anything!

Whilst we try to make everything in our dollshouses as close as possible to the real thing, we should also remember that it isn't actually being used in the same way as the full sized item, and is essentially a model. For instance, you don't need a fleecy backing on your bedcovers because nobody is going to actually snuggle down under the covers for a good night's sleep, and more importantly, the extra thickness will make your bedcover look out of proportion. You don't need to secure raw edges to prevent fraying as there is no wear and tear here. Clothing doesn't even have to fit, it is as useful hanging on the wardrobe door as it is on a figure.

I hope that by the end of this book you will be looking at the items in your home in a different way, and thinking 'now what could I make with that?'

Contents:

Chapter 1 - Socks

Chapter 2 - Woolly Gloves

Chapter 3 - Latex Gloves

Chapter 4 - Household Linen

Acknowledgements

Socks

Socks are a great source of material for making doll's house items, and it doesn't matter whether it's an old sock with a hole in the toe or a new one bought from a discount store.

If you take a closer look at a sock you'll see it's made of miniature knitting – fantastic for making jumpers and sweaters for all your doll's house family. It's also a soft 'cuddly' fabric so it's great for home furnishings such as throws, bed covers, blankets, etc. Many socks these days have fun designs and pictures you can utilise for cushions, bed spreads (particularly children's) and playmats. In fact once you get started the possibilities are endless…

Basic Blanket

All you need is...

- A sock
- Clear tape
- Scissors
- Wire or sandwich bag ties (optional)

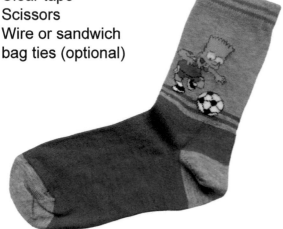

Step. 1

Cut a square or rectangle of fabric from your sock, there is no set size requirement it just depends on the size of your sock and the pattern on it, if there is one. As a guide the blanket shown here is 9cm x 10cm.

Step. 2

Next you will need some clear sticky tape. On the reverse side of your fabric carefully tape around the edges.

You need to cover about 1cm all around the edge. This can be a bit fiddly and with standard size tape it is sometimes easier to actually stick your fabric to the table and cut off the excess tape afterwards.

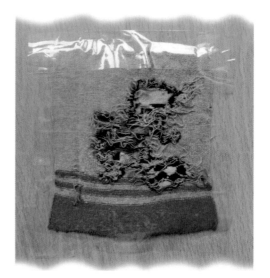

This way once you have done one side it is held in place on the table and doesn't move about so much whilst you are doing the other sides.

When you have done all four sides remove your fabric from the table and trim around the edges so that there isn't any tape visible from the front, whilst doing this also round off the corners of your blanket.

Step. 3

Using a pair of sharp scissors very carefully snip around the edge of the blanket to form a fringe. Add in a few 'V' shaped snips as you go around the corner so that your fringe isn't an odd shape, and put in a few 'V' shaped snips here and there to make the fring stand out along the straight edges. The depth of the fringe should be about the same as the depth of the tape.

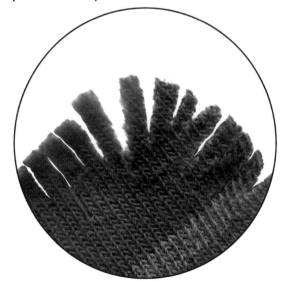

Step. 4

It is possible to make these blankets without using the tape but it would mean that your fringe would be very delicate, if just one 'tassel' comes off it could spoil your whole blanket. However, the tape can tend to make the fringe curl up so it's a good idea to 'press' it under a book or heavy object overnight.

If you want your blanket to 'drape' as the one pictured here over a chair, simply tape some wire (or sandwich bag ties) to the back of the blanket and use this to form it into the shape you want.

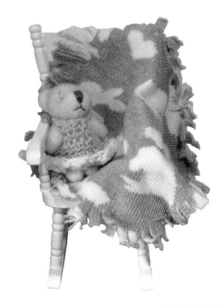

Bed throw

All you need is...

- A sock
- Scissors
- Double-sided sticky tape
- Wire (sandwich bag ties) optional

This is a quick and easy way to smarten up a bed set, especially when displayed with a matching cushion.

Step. 1

For a single bed; cut a straight cross-section from your sock about 7cm wide, then cut down one side to open out the fabric leaving you with a rectangle 7cm wide and usually around 15cm long.

An average sock will make a throw suitable for a single bed. If you'd like to make one for a double bed you would need a longer sock such as a knee high one to enable you to cut a rectangle approximately 7cm x 19cm. (Cut lengthways rather than a cross section).

Now from each corner cut a small square roughly 1cm by 1cm.

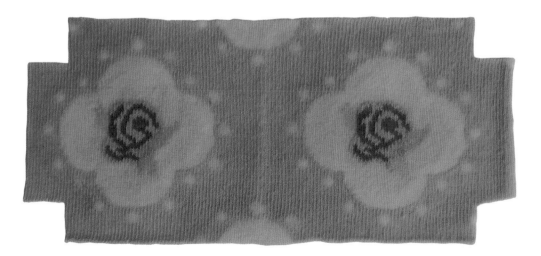

Step. 2

On the reverse side of your sock piece stick a narrow strip of double sided sticky tape along both of the long edges. If you are using standard inch wide tape you can cut it in half lengthways to give two narrow strips.

Working on one side at a time, peel off the backing strip. At this point it is a good idea to place a wire (or a couple of sandwich bag ties) onto the sticky strip as shown above, this enables you to position your throw perfectly over your miniature bed.

The wires (or sandwich bag ties) are optional but if you can get into the habit of adding wires like this the finished effect can be far more realistic looking.

Step. 3

This part can be a little fiddly! Carefully fold over and stick down the long edge of the sock piece in line with the squares that you have cut from the corners. Repeat the same procedure on the other side.

Step.4

Now all you have to do is snip a fringe along the shorter edges. Then position over the bed bending the wires to give a 'draped' effect.

A shorter version of these makes a good armchair back cover too.

Playmats

All you need is...

* A sock with a picture design
* Needle and thread
* Scissors

So far we have always split the sock open and used it like any other fabric, but for these playmats we don't need to open up the fabric as we want a double thickness material anyway and if we leave it whole it makes for a neater finish.

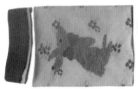

Step. 1

There is no pattern template for these as the size is governed by your particular sock, and the picture on it. Simply cut off the elasticated rib around the top of the sock leaving a flat straight edge across the top.

Then make another cut right across the sock underneath your picture or motif, taking care to leave enough material for a small hem top and bottom without spoiling your picture.

Step. 2

Now fold the fabric at the top inwards to form a hem, and tack in place. Repeat with the lower edge.

Then, using matching colour thread neatly oversew the top and bottom edges, remove the tacking stiches and lightly press.

Cushions

All you need is...

For the inner:
- Small piece of plain fabric
- Scrap of paper or card
- Tiny amount of filling
- Needle & thread
- Scissors

For the cover:
- A sock
- Needle & thread
- Scissors

You might think that making a cushion couldn't be simpler – you just sew two squares of fabric together, turn inside out, stuff and sew up the opening – and you'd be right, but there are two issues with this method that can leave you with a rather mis-shapen cushion. Firstly the corners won't be very square because when you turn the cushion inside out you have a gathering of excess fabric in the corners which will put them out of shape, and secondly when sewing up the opening it's very difficult to get a smooth edge, it usually curves inwards again spoiling the shape of your finished product.

However, this doesn't mean that there is anything at all wrong with making cushions in this manner, it does make them a very quick and easy project, but if you have the patience to spend a bit more time on it then the following method can give very good results.

Cushion Inner: Step. 1

First make a cushion inner; cut a square template (2.5 cm is a good size) out of paper or card, draw around it on a scrap of plain fabric and roughly cut out leaving a good seam allowance around the square. Place this on top of another piece of fabric to give a double thickness and using tiny running stitch or back stitch sew around three sides of the square (I've used a contrasting colour cotton just for demonstration purposes).

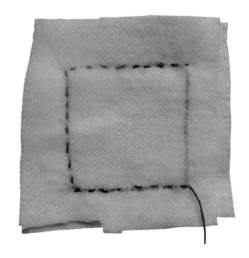

Step. 2

Next you need to fill your tiny cushion, there is no need to go and buy special filling material, cotton wool will do fine, or the stuffing out of an old pillow is perfect.

Step. 3

Now sew along the fourth edge of the square and trim the edges close to the stitching. Note that you do not turn this inside out as the firmer edges will give your finished cushion a better shape.

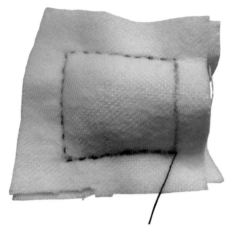

Cushion Cover: Step. 1

Trace or copy the template overleaf and cut out, also cut out the dotted square in the middle to create a 'window'.

Cut your sock so that you can open up the fabric and lay it flat. Position the template so that the picture or motif you want to be on the cushion is showing through the window.

Draw around the outer rectangle and cut out the fabric (do not mark inside the window, this is just to help you position the template on your sock fabric).

Step. 2

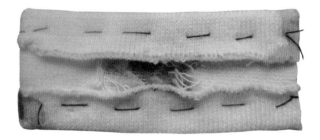

Fold the two long sides of your rectangle over to form a 1cm hem and tack in place. Now with the design inwards fold the strip in half and sew the raw edge from top to bottom using backstitch to form a small tube.

Turn the tube the right way out and flatten, placing the seam at centre back so that your design is showing in full.

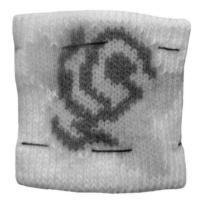

Step. 3

With matching cotton carefully oversew along the top edge of the cushion. Next, insert your cushion inner making sure that all the seams inside the cover are laying flat.

Finally, oversew along the bottom edge of the cushion (you should need to stretch the fabric a little to fit properly over the inner) and remove the tacking threads.

There are pattern templates for a small cushion and a larger 'scatter' cushion, both are made in the same way.

Templates for cushion inners

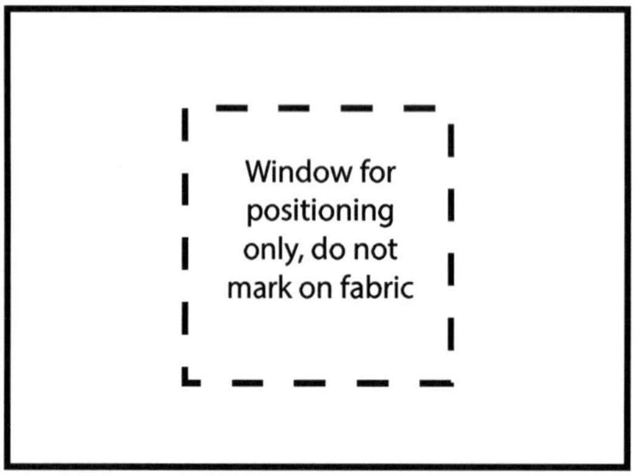

Small Cushion

Scatter Cushion

Templates for cushion covers

Window for positioning only, do not mark on fabric

Small cushion

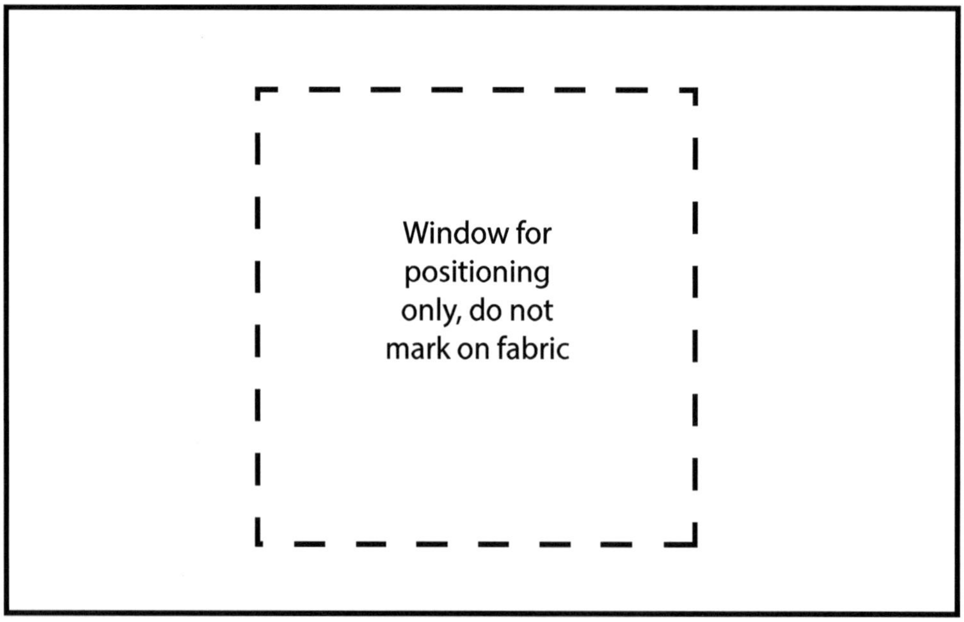

Window for positioning only, do not mark on fabric

Scatter cushion

Bath mats & rugs

Easy: ⭐⭐⭐⭐⭐

All you need is...

- A fluffy sock, such as a bedsock
- A piece of card (cereal box)
- Double-sided sticky tape
- Needle or pin
- Scissors

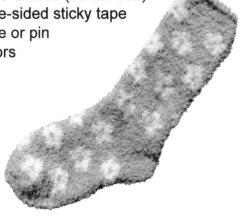

Step. 1

Prepare your sock by cutting it open so that you have a flat piece of material big enough for your chosen rug or mat shape.

Cut your rug shape from the card, you can use the templates overleaf or make up your own shape.

Step. 2

Now, using the double-sided sticky tape completely cover one side of your cardboard piece leaving a little extra over the edges as well (too much is better than not enough here).

Don't peel off the backing paper just yet, and take care not to overlap the tape as this makes it difficult to remove the backing strip.

Step. 3

Trim the excess sticky tape around your rug shape but leave about 2mm over all around the edge. Now peel off the backing paper (this is sometimes harder than it sounds!). Gently press the 2mm excess tape over the edge of the cardboard shape.

Then using the pin or needle, work your way around the edge of your rug just catching the material and pulling it over the edge.

Step. 4

Place the card shape, sticky side down, onto the reverse side of your sock fabric being aware of any pattern and lining it up with your shape. Press the shape firmly down onto the material, and cut around it, cutting right next to the card edge.

If your sock fabric is stripey it's a good idea to try and ensure the edges of your rug end 'mid-stripe' as this gives a better finished look.

Step. 5

Finish by rolling your fingers over the edges pressing the fabric onto the 2mm excess of sticky tape and giving a neat edge to your rug.

18

Rug & Bath Mat Templates

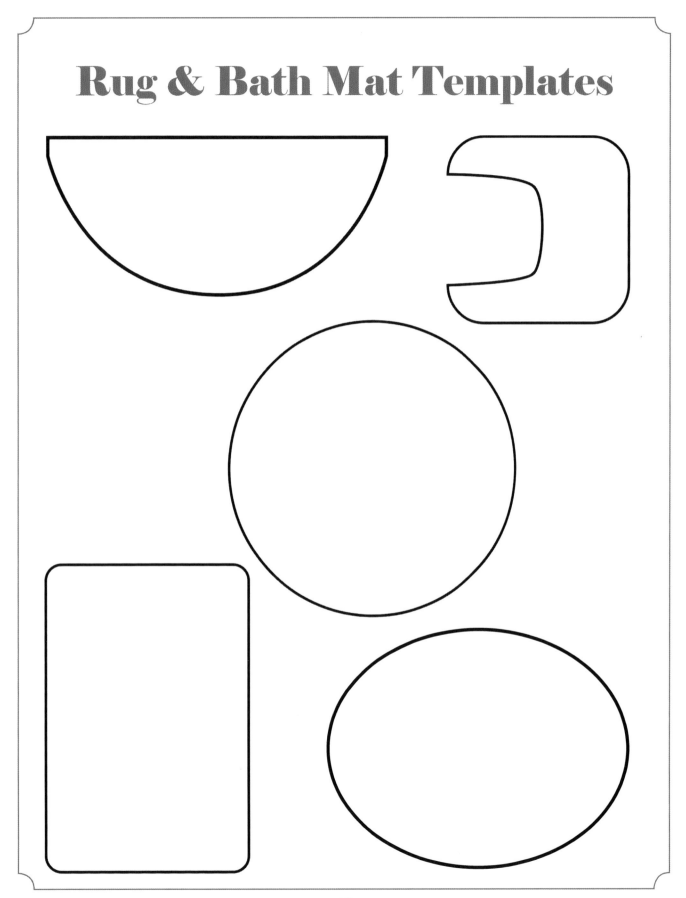

Bedcover

All you need is:...

- A sock
- Length of ribbon
- Needle & thread
- Wire or sandwich bag ties
- Scissors

Makes a great picnic rug too!

Sock bedcovers are a bit fiddly to make but with a bit of patience the finished item is well worth it. They are great for childrens bedrooms as so many socks have cool character designs on, so you could have a modern themed bedroom and keep up with the latest craze!

Your length of ribbon needs to be about half a metre long and 15mm wide, this sounds very specific but any narrower and your hem would be too delicate and although you could use ribbon a little wider, if you go too large your bedcover edge will look out of proportion. You could also use bias binding.

Step. 1

First cut your bedcover piece out of your sock, I haven't provided a template as it is governed by the size of your sock and any pattern on it, but it needs to be either square or rectangular with neat straight sides and corners.

As a guide the one pictured here is 10cm x 11cm.

Step. 2

Taking the length of ribbon carefully iron it in half lengthways. This is quite tricky to do but will make it much easier to attach to your bedcover.

Beginning in the middle of the bottom edge of your cover tack the ribbon around the edge 'sandwiching' the sock material in the fold of the ribbon.

Insert the wire, or sandwich bag ties, into the ribbon edging as you go. This is to allow you to shape the bedcover over the bed for a natural look so it doesn't need to be a continuous wire all the way around, I have just put a piece on the top and bottom edges up to the corners.

For a neatly folded corner tack right up to the edge of the material, then come back a stitch to bring the cotton back, fold the ribbon up the next edge and tack the folded corner in place.

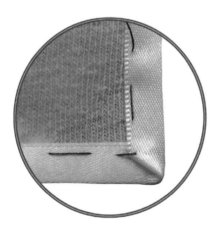

When you are almost completely round, snip the length of ribbon so that you have approximately a 1cm overlap to where you first started and continue tacking right over the overlap.

I tried several different methods of finishing here such as folding the ribbon edge over in a hem but I found that the best finish was actually made by doing nothing - just cut off the ribbon.

Step. 3

With thread matching the ribbon colour, sew tiny stitches carfully catching in just the very edge of the ribbon. Making sure you have sewn through the ribbon edge on the back as well as the front of the bedcover continue all the way around. I have used a contrasting colour here to demonstrate but with matching thread your stitches should almost disappear.

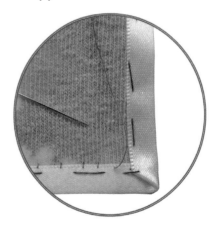

Remove the tacking stitches and press your finished item through a damp cloth.

Bedcover, or a picnic rug?

Ponchos

Easy: ★★★★★

All you need is...

- A sock
- Pen and ruler
- Scissors
- Decoration (optional)

So quick and easy to make!

Step. 1

Once again there is no pattern template for these ponchos as the exact shape of the sock heel will vary. Instead we are going to use a couple of simple measurements; from the centre of the curve of the heel measure 7cm in each direction and make a small mark with a pen. Then measure across the sock 5cm from the centre of the heel and leave another mark (there is usually a line to follow for this where the stitches of the sock material turn around the heel). Join your marks together using a ruler or other straight edge. (I have drawn quite a dark line but this is purely for demonstration purposes, you only need the line to be just visible). Cut along the lines.

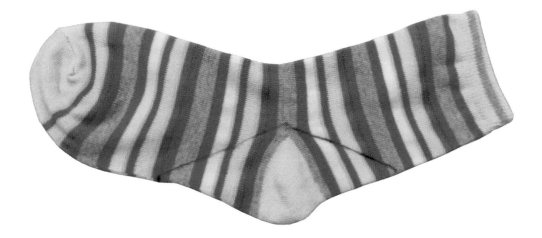

You can just use this one cut, or you can add a second cut on the front of the poncho from the centre of the neck downwards.

Step. 2

Open your heel segment up and fold in half the other way so that the two sharper points are together. Now just trim the corners off the 'shoulders' of your poncho. I've marked where to cut here but there is no need to actually draw this on yours just snip a little off the corner and round off the lower points of the poncho too.

Step. 3

To make the neck opening make a small cut across the top of the heel where I have marked here, again there is no need to actually draw this line on the poncho. Be careful not to make this cut too large (you can always make it bigger if needed but you can't reverse it if it's too large) as you don't want it to slip off the shoulders of your doll.

Step. 4

Carefully snip a fringe around the edge and your poncho is complete.

The beauty of dolls house people is that they aren't very hard wearing on clothing! So it's perfectly fine to leave a 'raw' edge as it is unlikely to fray or run unless you dress and undress your dolls all the time.

However, if you prefer a more finished look work around the neck opening in tiny blanket stitch using one strand of embroidery thread and add a couple of strands, maybe with a small bead on the end, for the ties.

V-neck jumper

All you need is...

- A sock
- Needle & thread
- Scissors & a pen
- Tracing paper

A V-neck jumper is ideal for the man of the home and with plenty of suitable men's sock patterns and colours to choose from you can make anything from a patterned golf style jumper to a plain grey jumper from a boy's school sock.

These are relatively simple to make but for best results use a thinner (cheaper) sock as jumpers made from good quality denser material can look a bit too chunky.

Don't forget that jumpers don't have to be shown being worn, they make great display pieces just hanging on a cupboard.

Step. 2

Place your two body pieces with right sides together, and sew one shoulder seam from C to D using tiny backstitch.

Step. 1

Trace or copy the pattern pieces shown overleaf, cut them out and using them as templates cut the pieces out of your sock.

You will also need to cut off the ribbed top of the sock (and snip this open as shown). This will be used for the neckband (don't worry we'll trim it to size later).

Step. 3

You now need to sew the ribbed edging strip along the neck opening from A to B to C to A. To do this place the right side of the front piece, edge A-B, so that it is overlapping the ribbed strip by just a few millimetres with the cut edge of the ribbing strip uppermost. It's worth studying the picture here for a few seconds to make sure you're sewing in the right place!

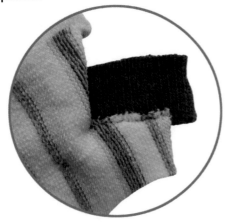

Carefully sew with very small stitches along the V of the front of the jumper (from A to B to C) opening the 'V' out so that it's a straight line along the ribbing. Then over the shoulder seam at C and across the back of the neck to point A.

Trim of the excess material from the ribbed strip.

Step. 4

Sew the other shoulder seam, from D to A including the neckband. And sew a small dart in the rib material at the bottom of the V neck to help it lay neater.

Step. 5

Now open out your garment and, with right sides facing, sew the sleeve pieces to the body from E via D to E.

At the lower edge of both the sleeves and the body pieces fold and sew a small hem (about 6mm).

Step. 6

With the right side inward fold your garment in half and sew from the wrist, past the armpit and down to the bottom hem (F to E to G). Repeat for the other side.

To sew the hem make the tiniest stitch you can manage on the main side and then make a 'normal' stitch in the folded edge, and repeat. Unlike the rest of your sewing these stitches should not be very tight as any tension in the thread will cause the stitches to be visible from the front.

Finally, turn your jumper the right way out and put on your doll (head first is usually best so as not to stretch the neck). Or why not hang it on the wardrobe door for display?

You can make great Christmas jumpers too!

V-neck Jumper

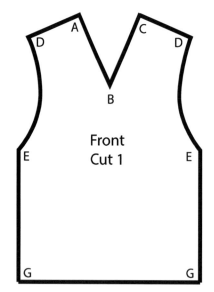

Front
Cut 1

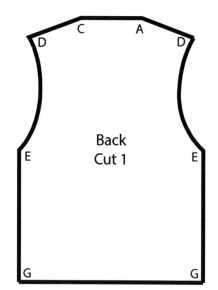

Back
Cut 1

Pattern Templates

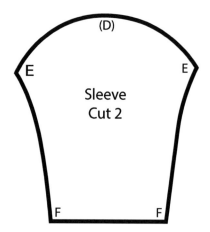

Sleeve
Cut 2

Ladies Jumper

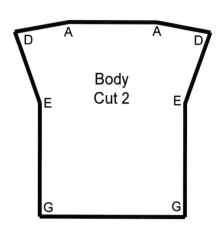

Body
Cut 2

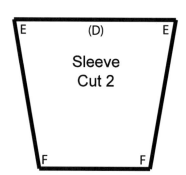

Sleeve
Cut 2

Ladies Jumper

All you need is...

- A sock
- Tracing paper
- Scissors & a pen
- Needle & thread
- Decoration (optional)

A little decoration can make all the difference to a plain jumper

Step. 1

Trace or copy the pattern pieces on the previous page and, using them as a template cut out the pieces from your sock.

Incidentally, the blue jumper pictured here is made from the foot part of the sock used to make the basic blanket at the beginning of the chapter, so don't be too quick to throw away any parts that you haven't used.

Step. 2

Take the two body pieces, with right sides together, and sew across the shoulder seams from A to D using tiny backstitch. (Sew both shoulders).

Next, open the two body pieces out and turn a small hem around the neck edge. As with the V neck jumper sew the hem by making the tiniest stitch possible on the fabric that will be visible and then make a 'normal' stitch in the folded edge, and repeat. Taking care not to make these stitches too tight as any tension in the thread will cause the stitches to show.

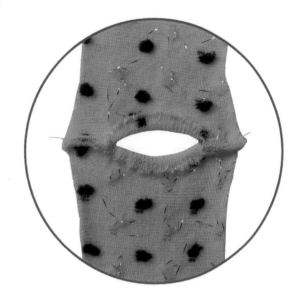

Step. 4

Fold the garment in half so that the body pieces are facing together again, and using backstitch, sew from the wrist past the armpit to the bottom edge (F to E to G).

Step. 3

Using backstitch attach the sleeve pieces to the main body, sewing from E to D to E. You might find it useful to make a small mark on the reverse of each sleeve piece at point D to help you position the sleeve centrally.

Using the same hemming method as for the neck opening, turn a small hem (about 6mm) on the bottom edge of the body pieces and on the wrist edge of the sleeves.

Turn the right way out and your jumper is complete (unless you wish to add some decoration).

These lovely little jumpers can make very cute Chrsitmas decorations too!

Don't underestimate the value of using clothing as accessories in your dolls house, a cardigan draped around the back of a chair, pyjamas on the bed or a jumper hanging on the wardrobe all help to give your house that 'lived in' look.

To achieve the casual look you will need to use small wires (as before sandwich bag ties are ideal) placing them inside your garment so that you can fashion the item into a natural looking pose, without this, because the garments are so small they tend to look a bit stiff and awkward. Simply insert the wire up the sleeve and fold it down into the body area and repeat on the other side, then you can bend the whole item into position and it will hold in place.

Woolly Gloves

In a cupboard, under the stairs, or tucked away somewhere I'm sure we all have a collection of hats, scarves and single woolly gloves, kept in the hope that the other glove will one day turn up. Well, a sure fire way of making sure the other glove turns up is to cut up the one you've got!

On the other hand, (excuse the pun) if you are more organised than I am and don't have any spare gloves about then they are easily found quite cheaply in a charity shop or discount store.

Woolly gloves are best for these projects but some items can be made from fleece or textile ones with good results too.

Hats

All you need is...

- A glove fingertip
- Needle & thread
- Pom poms, beads, etc to decorate
- Scissors

You can make a matching scarf too!

Step. 1

Taking a woolly glove cut off a finger (or thumb) about 4cm down.

But for either method you need to be aware that the hat will need to stretch slightly to fit on a dolls head, so if sewing you need to use backstitch to allow a bit of 'give', and if gluing you must not glue a continuous strip but leave small gaps to allow the fabric some movement.

Step. 2

With your thumbs on the inside hold the cut edge and pull outwards gently to encourage the fabric to curl. Once you've got it started roll the base up to form a fluffy band and secure in place with a few tiny stitches. If sewing really isn't your thing you can use a couple of very small dabs of glue instead.

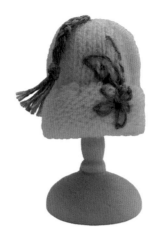

Step. 3

All that remains now is to decorate your hat, the possibilities for this are endless so have some fun experimenting. Here I have just added a pom pom.

Lazy Daisy Stitch

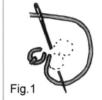

Fig.1

Make a knot in the end of your thread or attach thread to the back of your fabric.
Draw the needle and thread through the fabric at the centre point of your intended daisy.

Make a loop with the thread and insert the needle back through the centre of the flower (do not push the needle all the way through yet), now bring the point of

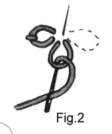

Fig.2

the needle up at the far edge of the petal inside the loop, see Fig.1.
Make a small stitch over the thread to hold the petal in place, and bring the point of the needle back through the centre of the daisy ready to begin the next petal, see Fig 2.

In the picture above the hatband has been folded rather than rolled to give a smarter look, and then decorated with a few beads. This is simple but effective and quite a 'chic' finish.

The picture top right shows a hat with a tassel rather than a pom pom, this has been made by plaiting embroidery thread. It also has a simple embroidery pattern of a flower done in Laisy Daisy stitch (detail opposite) and then a leaf and stem done in backstitch.

The blue hat above has been very simply decorated by gluing on some tiny sequins, you can find some great ones used for nail art.

Scarves

All you need is...

* A glove finger
* Scissors
* pom poms
  (optional)

Step. 1

Cut the finger from your glove from the base of the finger. Then carefully cut off the edges of the finger as shown below, leaving a narrow strip with a fold in the middle.

Step. 2

Gently pull the finger piece to encourage the edges to curl inwards. And that's it! You can leave your scarf with a raw edge at the bottom or maybe gather the lower edge and add a pom pom.

Having the fold in the middle helps it sit nicely on your doll, or hang as an accessory.

Muffs

Moderate:

All you need is...

- A glove finger
- Wool, cord or ribbon
- Decorations
- Needle & thread
- Scissors

To make a traditional muff couldn't be simpler and it's a great accessory both on a doll or hanging on a coat hook.

There are two sets of instructions, the first method is just slightly easier and doesn't require any sewing.

Rolled edge muff

Step.1

Cut a 4 - 5cm section from a glove finger and carefully stretch outward the cut edges to encourage them to roll. Once started, roll them over little more and either just leave in place, which is fine if using the muff as a fixed accessory i.e. hanging over a chair back, or you could add a few small dabs of glue inside the roll if you wanted it to be a bit more secure.

Step. 2

Thread a piece of wool, cord or thin ribbon, roughly 15cm long, through the finger section and tie the ends together in a knot making a loop that is about 5cm long from the knot to the mid point of the loop. Trim off the excess cord and bring the finger section around over the knot, so that it is hidden inside the muff.

If you're using wool for your neckcord and it doesn't seem quite enough, try using a crochet hook, or finger knitting to make a long chain for a cord as shown here.

Step.3

Decorate as you wish, I've simply glued on a few sequins but you could embroider or glue on any desgin you like.

Why not make a matching hat and muff set?

To display your doll using her muff you will have to partake in a little bondage! - Put one arm through the muff, and then tie the hands together with a little cotton or embroidery thread.

The hands don't need to quite touch, so don't worry if your doll doesn't really bend, you just need enough to hold them in a little, and then bring the muff down the arm and over the hands (covering the shackles!).

Smooth edge muff

Step. 1

For a more finished look, and if you don't mind a bit of sewing, cut a section from a glove finger about 4 - 5cm long, and turn the piece inside out.

Fold back the cut edges to form a hem and oversew in place picking up just the tiniest of stitches from the inside so that your sewing won't show on the right side. Turn the finger section back the right way out.

Step. 2

Add a neckcord as in the first method by taking a length of thin ribbon or cord about 15cm long and threading through the finger section.

Knot the ends together so that you have a loop that is about 5cm from the knot to the mid point of the loop.

Cut off any excess cord and bring the finger section around so that the knot is hidden inside.

A smart neckcord can make all the difference so try out some different materials, the one shown here is made from plaited embroidery thread.

Step. 3

Decorate your muff by adding beads, sequins, etc. I have sewn a small bow using the same embroidery thread as I used for the cord. The pom poms are made from coloured pipecleaners, simply cut a 2cm length and using long nosed pliers or pointed scissors wind the pieces into a tiny ball.

Dollybags

All you need is...

- A glove finger
- A bit of lace or braid
- Cotton wool or filling
- Small piece of cord or wool
- Needle & thread
- Scissors
- Thin ribbon, etc to decorate

Step. 1

From your glove finger cut off the tip about 2.5 cm down.

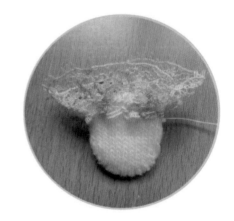

Take an oddment of lace or braid 10cm long and sew a line of running stitch along the straight edge (i.e. not the fancy edge).

Pulling carefully on the thread gather up your lace until it is just long enough to fit around the cut edge of your glove fingertip.

Sew the lace around the edge of the fingertip as pictured with the fancy edge facing upwards, but don't cut the thread off just yet.

Step. 2

Make a loop from a piece of wool, cord, ribbon, etc. with a knot about 4cm from the top of the loop. Take a small amount of wadding and wrap it into a ball around the knot of the loop.

This is the bag handle and can make a big difference to the finished look so think carefully about colour and style. I have used plaited embroidery thread in a contrasting colour, but you could use thin ribbon or cord, or even pretty wool.

Step. 3

Push the ball of wadding into the fingertip, leaving the loop sticking out.

Now, with the thread that is still attached, sew around the 'neck' of the bag (immediately under the lace) pulling the stitches tightly as you go to gather in the neck of the bag. Fasten off.

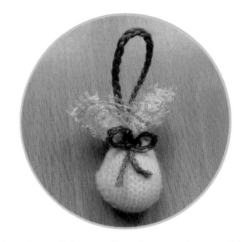

gradually pull it smaller than to try and fiddle with a tiny piece of ribbon.

You could also add some beads, sequins or glitter for that extra sparkle.

Step. 4

Decorate your bag as you wish. Here I have tied the neck of the bag with embroidery thread to match the handle and sewn it into a bow.

If you are using ribbon to tie a bow around the bag it is easier to tie a larger bow and

Teacosies

All you need is...

- A glove finger
- Needle & thread
- Decorations
- Scissors

Step. 1

Cut the finger tip from your glove judging the length by measuring the height of your teapot and adding 1cm.

Using a sharp pair of scissors cut a small, vertical slit either side of the finger piece just below the rounded top. This is for the handle and spout to stick through.

To get the neatest edge try to make your cut as straight as possible in line with the grain of the knitted fabric. You can just leave these cuts with a raw edge as the knitted material shouldn't fray out, or you can add a little PVA glue or clear nail enamel to the openings to seal them.

Step. 2

Turn your finger tip inside out and fold up a small hem. It is best to sew this place by oversewing the hem just picking up the tiniest stitch from the inside so that the stitches don't show on the front. If you aren't keen on sewing you could simply add a few spots of PVA glue inside the hem and leave to dry.

Now turn your cosy the right way out and decorate however you wish.

These little teacosies are really cute and so simple to make. They are also 'made to measure' so you can make a cosy for any of your teapots or even for a coffee pot.

There are endless ways to decorate them, but here are a few ideas...

Here I have simply added a flower sequin with a bead in the centre and another matching bead on the top. Any design with beads and/or sequins can be either sewn or glued in place.

For my coffee pot I have glued a bright red pom pom on the top and using a matching colour wool sewn random small stitches over the cosy being careful not to pull the stitch too tight and to leave the wool just a little proud to give a bobbly effect.

Using backstitch I have simply sewn 3 lines of zig zags in different bright colours using 2 strands of embroidery thread, and finished off with a cute bobble on top. Or you could embroider the lazy daisy stitch as shown on page 35.

Petbeds

All you need is...

- A glove
- PVA or 'tacky' glue
- A plastic milk bottle top
- Small piece of card
- A 2p coin (or similar)
- Needle & thread (optional)

These little petbeds are a great use of the elasticated wristband part of a glove, but you need a glove with a folded over wristband as the rim of these baskets is the folded edge.

Step. 1

First cut the wristband off the glove so that you have a tube like a sports wristband. This elasticated or ribbed fabric will be folded over to give a nice edging on the wrist. If the folded fabric is sewn together carefully snip it apart. Now unfold the tube so that it is twice as long and the fold line runs around the centre.

Step. 2

Place your lid, on it's side, with the flat edge (the top) on the centre of the fold line, now mark the fabric on the other side of the lid. Roll the lid along and mark again. Repeat this until you have enough marks to join into a line, as shown. Cut along this line.

Step. 3

With the newly cut edge of the fabric uppermost, insert your bottle top into the tube of fabric with the inside of the lid facing upwards. Push the lid into the tube until the fold line of the fabric is level with the rim of the lid, so you should have approximately 1cm of fabric over the top. (Don't worry about the excess fabric underneath the bottle top at this point.)

Apply some glue to the inside of the bottle top rim and fold the fabric down into the glue. Gently press the edges in place inside the lid. Leave to dry.

Step. 4

Whilst that is drying make the cushion for the bed: Cut a section of fabric (roughly 7cm by 6cm) from the palm of your glove. On a small piece of card (cereal box will do) draw around a 2p piece and cut out. Place your circle of card in the middle of your palm fabric and sew a circle of running stitch about 1/2 cm wider than your cardboard disc, don't fasten off the thread yet.

Trim the fabric just outside of the stitching line, being careful not to cut your thread.

Step. 5

Now, holding the cardboard disc firmly in place pull up your stitches so that the fabric gathers around the disc, and fasten off securely.

If you're really not keen on sewing this can be done by snipping the fabric around the cardboard disc so that it looks a bit like a fringe, and then gluing each 'tab' onto the disc one by one. However, this can be quite fiddly so sewing here is actually the simpler option.

Step. 6

To finish off the bed, roughly trim off the excess fabric (hanging underneath the lid), then gently pull the fabric away from the

side of the lid and apply some glue to the side edge of the plastic lid, let the fabric fall back in place against the glued side, and again, leave to dry.

Once completely dry trim off any remaining excess fabric so that your petbed sits flat on the floor. Now insert your cushion and Pet!

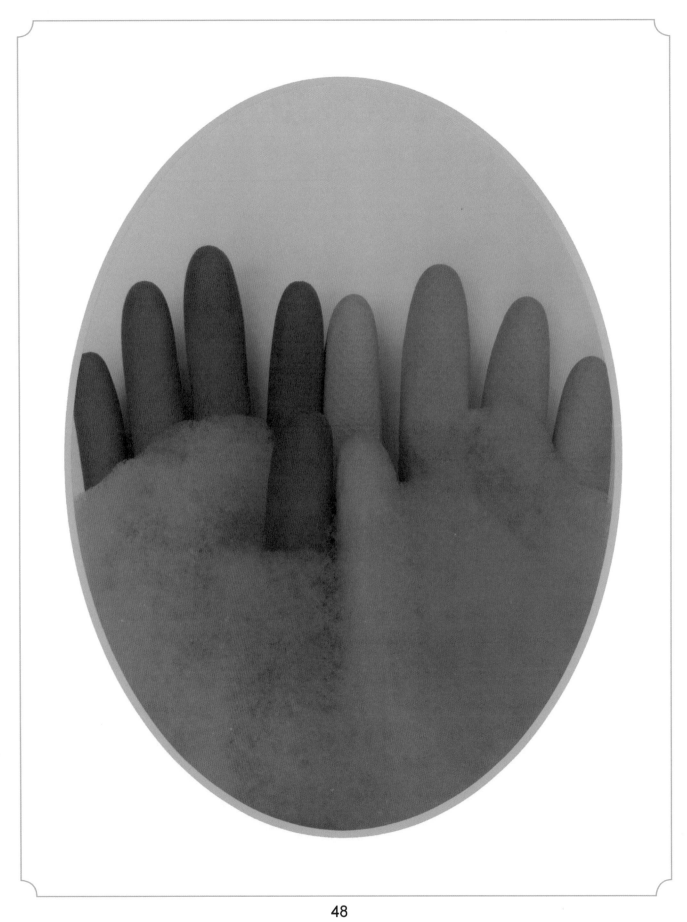

Latex Gloves

Latex gloves provide a great source of material for many different projects. Medium or small sized gloves work well for all these projects and for most projects the thinner (cheaper) gloves give a better finish and are easier to work with.

Keep an eye out when you're shopping and you'll be amazed at how many different colours washing up gloves are now available in, I have found yellow (obviously), pink, mauve, green, red, blue, peach and even black ones.

Many of these projects literally take just a few minutes to make and need nothing more than a couple of cuts with a sharp pair of scissors, however, it is a very different fabric to use and may take a few practice runs to get the hang of working with it so I would recommend buying a couple of pairs of gloves so you have twenty fingers to play with and expect to waste a couple!

It's always a good idea to read through all the instructions before you begin any project.

Beach bags

All you need is...

- A latex glove finger
- A small piece of string, cord or wool
- A needle (large enough to thread the string through)
- Scissors

These cute bags can be made in minutes!

Step. 1

Cut the fingertip off the glove 3cm from the tip. Have a good look at your glove section, you will often find that the fabric is not all smooth and that there is a textured section.

Use this to your advantage to give some pattern to your bag, so position the textured area either down the centre of your bag or down the sides as you wish.

Step. 2

Cut two pieces of string (or you could use cord or wool) approximately 15cm long. This is longer than you need but easier to work with.

Taking the first piece of string make a knot in one end and trim off any excess string below the knot.

Thread the string onto the needle.

Step. 3

Insert the needle into the front of the bag, ½ cm in from the right and ½ cm down from the cut edge of the fingertip, pull the thread through to the knot.

Repeat with the other piece of string on the other side of the bag, taking care to make sure that your bag handles are both the same length, and your bag is complete.

These bags look better with things in them, so try rolling up a tiny square of fabric to look like a towel and maybe add a tiny drinks bottle or pair of flip flops if you have them. It also helps to just add a bit of packing in the bottom of the bag, a piece of scrunched up cling film is ideal.

Then insert the needle from the inside of the fingertip ½ cm in from the left and ½ cm down from the top and bring the string back through to the front of the bag.

Remove the needle and adjust the handle to the length you require. Make a little mark on the string where it comes back through the bag using a biro or felt pen, then pull the string further through and make a knot over your mark, trim off any excess and pull the handle up until the knot is preventing it going any further.

Waste Bins

All you need is...

- A suitable lid (see below)
- A large button
- A latex glove finger
- Scissors
- Decoration if required

> *These little waste bins are so simple to make and are a great accessory.*

Firstly, you need to find a suitable lid, it needs to be quite narrow, between 20 and 25 mm and the top must flat as this is the base that it will stand on. The best ones I have found are the clear protective lids from spray bottles for cosmetics, lotions or sun cream, but check the lids of your perfume or aftershave bottles too.

Secondly, you need a button to fit your lid. This needs to be the same diameter or just slightly larger as this will become the lid for your waste bin. Don't worry if your button has holes, etc. for sewing on, we will look at this later. If you don't think you have a suitable size button check any jackets or clothes with larger buttons on as these often have a spare on the inside that you could use. Still no luck? - you could even use a coin or a button badge, maybe you have some spare foreign coins that are no use to you now?

Step 1.

Cut the finger from your latex glove at the base of the finger to allow you plenty of fabric to work with, the little finger is usually best for these as you need quite a snug fit, if the fabric is stretched around the lid the end result will be neater.

Push the lid into the finger as far as it will go, you should be left with a little 'bubble' at the fingertip. If your fabric is quite thin you can simply make a tiny cut to release the air from the bubble and push the lid further down stretching the fabric until the base is smooth (pictured in yellow).

Or, if your fabric is a little thicker and seems unlikely to stretch enough to be flat you will need to make a slightly larger cut; using a pair of sharp pointed scissors carefully cut a small circle around the bubble leaving just a little fabric edge around the top of the lid (pictured in blue).

and your cut edge should just stretch over the rim of the lid leaving a neat top edge.

Step 3.

The lid for your waste bin is simply your button! But look at it carefully to see how to use it to its best advantage; some buttons have a solid 'loop' underneath for sewing through – this can look like a handle on your bin lid, or maybe the top side looks better? For buttons with holes right through you could glue some beads over the holes to make an attractive design, or maybe thread a loop of ribbon through?

If required, decorate with tiny stickers or transfers, such as those used for nail art.

Step 2.

Now for the open end of your waste bin; if your fabric is thin you can simply cut the glove finger off about 1cm above the edge of the lid and fold fabric inside the lid. You can glue this in place if you wish but don't worry if the inside doesn't look brilliant as these bins are intended to have a lid on!

If your fabric is a bit thicker, gently pull the lid back up the finger just a fraction, literally no more than 2mm. Then carefully cut the glove finger flush with the top edge of the lid. Now push the lid back down into the fingertip

Handbags

All you need is...

- A latex glove (a thin 'cheap' one is easier to use for this)
- Small piece of card
- Masking tape
- PVA glue
- Scissors & a Pen

These are a bit fiddley, and take a lot of taping. But the end results are very effective!

Step 1

Using the 'body' part of the glove copy and cut two pieces of latex fabric using the large template and one piece with the small template. The larger pieces will become the front and back of your handbag so be aware of any patterning on the glove material and use it to your advantage.

Also cut two pieces of card using the small template.

Centrally place your small cardboard pieces on the back of the larger fabric pieces. Latex glove material can be surprisingly thin so if your cardboard pieces have writing, etc. on one side put this facing upwards so that it doesn't show through on your finished bag.

Small Template	Large Template

Step 2

Working on the longer side fold the fabric over the card and secure in place with a long thin strip of masking tape, you may find you need to cut the tape lengthways to get a thin enough strip.

Repeat the other side, making sure the masking tape does not go over the folded edges.

Repeat with the other piece of card and fabric and trim off any excess masking tape.

Put the two taped up pieces side by side so that the folded edges are almost touching, but not quite, and position the small fabric piece centrally across both pieces as shown. Tape in place.

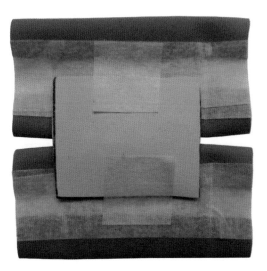

Step 3

One by one, fold the four raw edges at the sides over and secure with a small piece of tape, again keeping the tape away from the folded edges.

Step 4

Add your handle; some rubber gloves come with a 'rolled' lower edge and this makes an excellent handle for these little handbags, just cut a length as close as possible to the rolled edge.

Or you could use, cord, ribbon, plaited embroidery thread, etc. Whatever you are using secure it in position as shown with, you've guessed it, another piece of tape!

Step 5

Apply a sizeable blob of PVA glue inbetween the handle and up to the edges of the masking tape, then fold in half to make your bag. Remove any glue that has oozed out of the sides, then leave, weighted down, to dry.

The yellow bag above has made the most of the textured part of the glove giving an interesting finish, and has a small sequin on a tiny strip of fabric to look like a fastening.

Once dry, decorate as required. A couple of beads can look like a clasp on top, or you could glue in a thin strap and add a bead or decoration to look like a buckle fastening.

The handbag below has been decorated with transfers used for nail art.

The glove for this mauve coloured bag didn't have a rolled edge on the wrist, but it did have an attractive pattern instead that I've used here, but be wary of this type of pattern as you must have it level for it to look right.

The fluffly handle is a piece of pipe cleaner and the bow is a nail art decoration.

Using a Former

Regular
Former

Small
Finger
Former

For the next few projects I would suggest using a 'former'. Simply copy one of the templates opposite depending on which size you need, and cut this out of cardboard, a cereal box is ideal.

Insert this into the cut off glove finger when indicated in the project instructions. All this does is hold the finger piece in shape making it easier to cut.

It isn't a necessity and you may find you manage better without it once you get started. (Just follow the instructions but omit inserting the former.)

The formers are much longer than needed but this makes it easier to hold on to your miniature project whilst you are working on it.

Shoulder bags

All you need is...

Easy:

- A latex glove finger
- Piece of cord, chain, ribbon, etc.
- Beads, sequins, etc to decorate
- A former (if using)
- PVA or 'Tacky' glue
- Scissors & a pencil

These simple bags are for decoration only as they will be glued closed

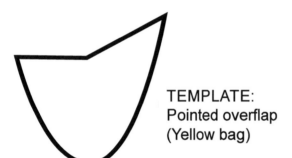

TEMPLATE:
Pointed overflap
(Yellow bag)

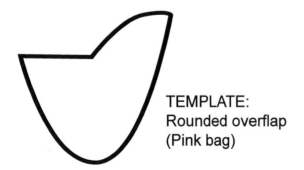

TEMPLATE:
Rounded overflap
(Pink bag)

Step 1

Cut the fingertip off your glove about 6 cm from the tip. Look at any patterning on your finger piece and insert the former so that the edges of the former are straight down the centre of the pattern (the edges will finish up as centre front and back of your bag).

Step 2

Copy one of the templates provided onto paper or card and cut out. Using this as a guide draw across the finger section on the former as shown opposite (I have used quite a dark line but this is for demonstration purposes, a very light pencil mark is all you need).

You may need to adjust the size to fit your particular finger; if your finger is wider place the template in the middle and extend the

Wrap a small amount of packaging, such as scrunched up cling film around the knot of the loop and push this inside the bag, making sure the handle is positioned so that it exits the bag either side of the overflap.

Step 4

Now fold the front flap of your bag over, through your handle loop, and glue in place.

cutting line equally either side. If it is smaller place the template so that it overhangs equally either side of the finger piece.

Using a sharp pair of scissors cut along the cutting line (you will need to cut through the glove and the former), then remove what is left of the former.

Step 3

Take your piece of cord, ribbon, etc. that you are using for the handle and tie a knot to make a loop that is slightly longer than the intended finished handle length. (Roughly 4 - 5 cm.)

Decorate with beads, sequins, etc. to finish.

Miniskirt

Very easy:

All you need is...

- A latex glove finger
- Scissors

These are probably the easiest thing to make in the entire book!

Step 1

Cut the fingertip off the glove, the example here is cut about 3cm from the tip for quite a short skirt, but you can really have any length skirt you like.

It's best to start a bit longer than you want as you can always shorten it but you can't make it longer!

Now cut just the tip of the finger off just after it starts to curve inwards, this will give the skirt a slightly smaller waist edge than hem edge.

And that's it, you're done!

Try experimenting with scissors that cut fancy edges to get a more interesting hem line, or maybe go for a longer skirt with an angled hem.

Halterneck top
(Pictured opposite)

All you need is...

- A latex glove finger
- A former (if using)
- Scissors & a pen

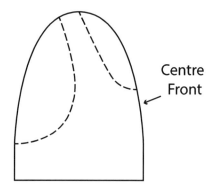

Centre Front

Step 1

Cut the finger off a glove approximately 4 ½ cm from the tip. It's important to be aware of any pattern or grip on your fingertip and make sure you use it to your advantage, for example if you have a vertical strip of pattern you could position it centre front, or down one side so that it looks as if it is all part of the design.

You can do this 'freestyle' without making the template if you wish. It's important to realise that these clothing projects are not an exact science and your cuts do not have to follow my suggestions exactly, have some fun experimenting as very slight changes can bring about different styles. (This is where the having extra fingers to play with comes in!)

Step 2

Place the 'former' inside the fingertip. Note that the edges of the former will be centre back and centre front, as you can see in the example here I have put the patterned area along the edge so it will become centre front when finished.

Copy or trace the diagram above to make a template, and using this, lightly draw the two dotted lines onto your glove fingertip.

Step 3

Now make your cuts (through both the finger and the former) making sure you cut over the lines so that there are no pen marks on your finished article. Remove top from former.

These tops are easiest put on the doll feet first as the shoulders can require a bit too much stretching to fit over.

Beach dress

Moderate:

All you need is...

- A latex glove finger
- Scissors & a pen
- 2 Formers (if using)

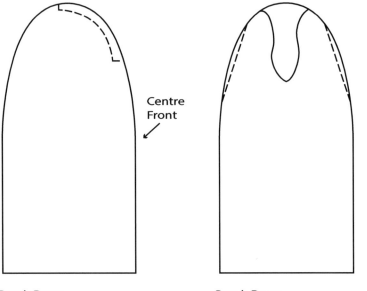

Centre Front

Beach Dress
Diagram 1.

Beach Dress
Diagram 2.

Step 1

Cut the finger from your glove approximately 7cm from the tip, you will probably need to use the middle finger for this and don't worry if you have to cut right at the base of the finger where it starts to get wider as this gives a nice 'flared' edge to the bottom of the dress.

Being aware of any pattern on your glove finger insert the former ready for the neck opening cut shown in Diagram 1.

Following the diagram lightly mark the dotted line on the finger with a pen. It doesn't need to be exactly the same, just use the diagram as a guide. If you are confident, you don't even need to actually draw the line you can just make the cut freehand.

Cut along the drawn line cutting through both the glove finger and the former. Remove the former.

Step 2

Now we are going to make the armhole cuts shown in the second Diagram.

Insert a new former into the glove finger but this time position the 'V' of the neck opening in the centre of the former as shown here.   If you aren't using a former you'll just need to re-fold your glove finger with the neck opening centre front.

A new dress in minutes!

Make the two armhole cuts shown in Diagram 2. These are very thin slashes, if you curve them too much you might find your doll is exposing more than she'd be comfortable with!

Be careful not to leave the shoulder straps too narrow as this piece needs to undergo a fair bit of stretching to fit on the doll so don't make it too delicate.

To finish off you could try cutting the bottom edge into a tiny fringe or decorate your dress using felt pens.

Swimsuit

Easy:

All you need is...

- A latex glove small finger
- Scissors & a pen
- 2 Formers (if using)
- Felt pens, etc to decorate (optional)

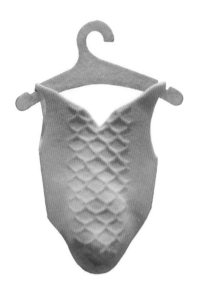

These swimsuits are 'made to measure' so first select the doll you are making the costume for. My dolls are all very skinny so the little finger of the glove is usually best as these costumes look better slightly stretched than baggy.

Step 1

Measure your doll from the crotch to the shoulder and take off 4mm, cut your glove finger to this length (if you aren't making this to actually put on a doll you need approximately 5cm).

Check the finger piece for any patterning or texture and if it has any decide where you'd like this to be on the swimsuit. I generally find that putting the pattern centre front looks best but you can also experiment with putting it to one side, or maybe you'd prefer it down the back out of sight?

Insert a former into the finger piece carefully positioning any texture area. At this point you might want to decorate your swimsuit using felt tip pen or biro (I have just outlined the textured area on the one shown here with felt pen).

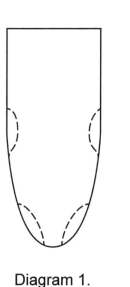

Diagram 1.

Step 2

Now, looking at the diagram make the cuts for the leg holes being careful not to leave too thin a 'gusset' as this can split easily when stretching the swimsuit onto the doll. (Sorry, sexy thong style costumes are out!)

It is better if you can manage to make these cuts freehand, but if you find it helpful just lightly draw on the fingertip copying the diagram but be careful to cut away all the pen mark.

Cut the armholes in the same way, as these swimsuits are made to measure I can't provide a template only a diagram, but you need to start your armhole cut about 3mm from the cut edge of the finger.

Step 3

Remove the former from the finger and insert a new former but this time with the edges of the former being centre front and centre back.

Trim the excess former that is sticking out of the top of the finger off. Make the cut for the back opening, over the shoulder and down to the centre front making sure it isn't too low!

Remove the former and put your finished swimsuit on the doll being careful not to pull the delicate straps more than necessary.

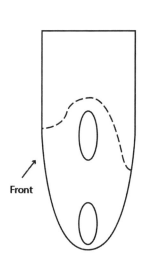

Front

Diagram 2.

The shoulder straps will 'flatten out' when the costume is stretched onto a doll (this is why we cut the finger 4mm shorter than needed). So if you are making your swimsuit for display purposes only you will need to trim the shoulder straps so that they are as thin as possible.

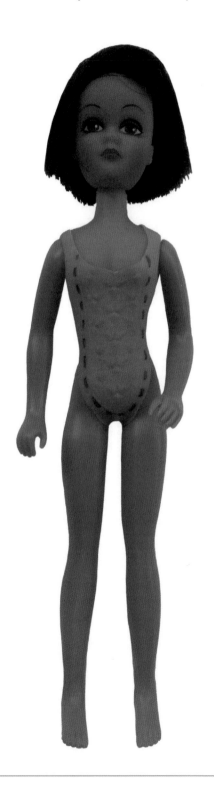

Swimhat

Swimhat diagram

If you'd like to make a swimhat simply cut the end off a latex glove finger approximately 3cm down and make an 'S' shaped cut following the diagram above.

These look best on short haired dolls or ones with hair suitable to plait down the back out of sight.

Sporty bikini

Easy: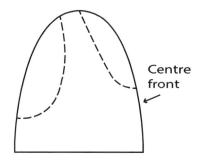

All you need is...

- Two latex glove fingers
- Scissors & a pen
- Two formers (if using)

Diagram 1.

Step 1

To make the bikini top follow the same instructions as for the Halter Neck Top on page 61 but using the fingertip of a glove cut just 3.5 cm from the tip and the bikini template (Diagram 1) above.

When the top is on the doll just fold up a small hem under the bust, doing this adds a bit of style to the bikini and avoids working with delicate straps etc. that might split when trying to put onto a doll.

Step 2

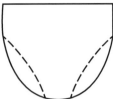

Diagram 2.

To make the bikini briefs cut the second finger 2 ½ cm from the tip and make the two leg hole cuts shown in Diagram 2 .

Put the pants on the doll and when in place just fold down a small hem as with the top.

There is no need to glue or fix the hem in place it should just stay put, and if you were to fix it, it would lose some of the flexibility and make it harder to stretch onto a doll.

Once you have mastered dressing your dolls with this fabric you may feel comfortable to cut the fingertips a little shorter and omit folding the hem, to give a less sporty style of bikini.

Unfortunately this item does not really work very well as a display item, it looks better on a doll.

Beach lilo

All you need is...

- A latex glove
- A sewing machine
- Matching coloured thread
- A piece of card
- Scissors and a pen
- Small amount of toy filling
- 3-5 drinking straws (approx 6mm diameter)

Lilo Template

Using a sewing machine with a latex glove can be fun. – It can also be very frustrating! So it's a very good idea to have a practice on a scrap piece of glove material before you start actually making anything. The smaller the stitch size the better, but keep an eye on the tension as this doesn't always appreciate tiny stitches and you may have to compromise with slightly larger stitches.

When using a sewing machine with this type of fabric it's important to be quite precise, we aren't going to be turning these lilos 'inside out' so all your stitching will be visible, as will the lines you draw around the template. Don't worry, this needn't be as bad as it sounds, you can see the lines but they don't spoil the item and you can obviously plan to have this side as the underneath.

Step 1

Copy the template onto a piece of card (cereal box is fine).

Making sure it is a least an inch longer than your card template cut the wrist section from the glove. If it has a rolled edge hem, cut this off too. But don't split the section lengthways or open it out, leave it as a 'tube'.

Being aware of any patterning on the fabric, and leaving some space all around, carefully draw the full template out as neatly as possible on your fabric bearing mind that this will be the underneath of your lilo. Having drawn the outer rectangle you may find it easier to add the other lines using a ruler.

Do not cut around the template lines at this stage.

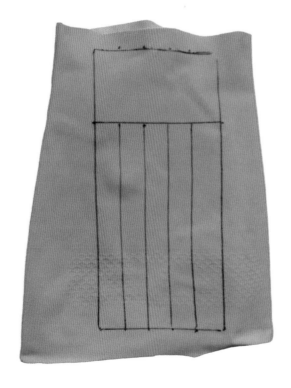

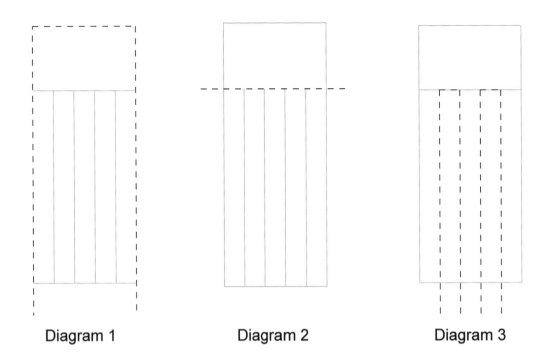

Diagram 1   Diagram 2   Diagram 3

Step 2

Sew around the three outer sides of your template as shown in Diagram 1. Sewing from, and to, the edge of the fabric i.e. past the template lines, as this will give a neater end result.

You may need to stretch the fabric taut as you sew to prevent it from puckering

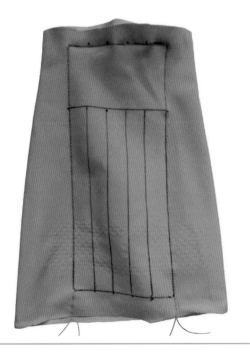

Step 3

Push some stuffing into the pillow end of the lilo making sure it is evenly distributed as you won't be able to adjust it later.

Then sew across the pillow line as shown in Diagram 2. Again, sewing to the edges of the fabric.

Step 4

Next sew up the centre lines as shown in Diagram 3.

Now cut around the three sides that were sewn following Diagram 1. Cut as close as you dare to the stitching leaving just 1mm of fabric over.

Step 5

Taking the drinking straws cut five 8.5cm lengths (you may be able to get two lengths from one straw) and push these into the grooves of the lilo right up to the pillow.

Finally, sew across the bottom line of the lilo and trim the edge to 1mm as before.

73

Raincoat

Trickier:

All you need is...

- A thin (cheap) latex glove
- Scissors & a pen
- A piece of card
- 4 Small beads or nail decorations
- All purpose polyurethane glue

These little coats are best made from really thin (cheap) latex gloves as the thinner material 'hangs' more naturally. Please note that these coats don't actually fasten, the 'buttons' are for effect only.

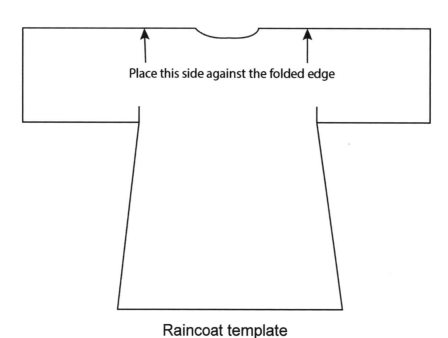

Place this side against the folded edge

Raincoat template

Step 1.

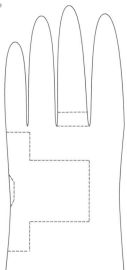

Copy the template onto a piece of card (cereal box is fine) and cut out.

Looking at the diagram above of the back of the glove, place the card template on the latex glove against the folded side of the wrist as indicated.

Cut out, cutting through the two thicknesses of the glove.

Don't forget the tiny 'overcuts' under the arms, and try to cut away any pen marks.

Step 2.

Open your coat piece out (it should look like a large cross) and place on the table with the inside of the material facing upwards, and the back (the side you drew on) nearest to you.

Take a felt tip pen or biro, a slightly chunky one is better if you can find one, and beginning at the edge nearest to you roll the fabric up to half way.

Place a thin line of glue along the cut edge of the sleeve on the pen as shown above, and then continue rolling so that the sleeve seam is glued together (if you're using a thinner pen try and match the sleeve edge so that it just overlaps enough to stick down).

Remove the pen when the glue is dry, and pull the back section of the raincoat down.

Step 3.

Now, on the inside edge of the front of the raincoat put a thin strip of glue down the side as shown. Carefully, stick this along the corresponding side of the back piece, overlapping the material similarly to the sleeve seams (don't worry if it doesn't match exactly at the bottom edge).

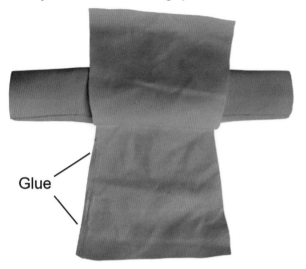

Glue

Repeat with the other side, and trim the bottom edge so that it is all uniform. Trim the sleeve ends as well if needed.

Cut a straight line up the centre front for the coat opening, if you aren't confident to do this freehand lightly draw a line with a sharp pencil using a ruler.

Step 4.

Now taking your original glove cut a section from the base of a finger, where the fabric starts to widen, about 1.5 cm wide as illustrated in the diagram on page 75. This is going to be the collar, turn it 'inside out'.

Find a piece of dowel, bottle top, or something to put the collar around (I've used a lipstick here) and put a thin line of glue around the narrower edge.

Starting with the centre back wrap the neck opening of your coat around the glued edge of the collar as shown in the picture. It is not likely to fit all the way around as you can see.

Step 5.

When the glue has dried remove the item holding the collar and trim off the excess collar section. Fold the collar over and depending on how thick your glove material is you might need to add a little bit of glue to hold it down.

Now just add your beads or decorations to look like buttons and with a pen or sharp pencil carefully draw on the corresponding buttonholes on the other side.

You may find there is a small 'gap' under the armpit, don't worry about this as it won't be seen, and it allows the fabric to hang more naturally.

If you are wanting to display your finished coat hanging on a hook, you may need to either use something such as 'tacky wax' to hold the sleeves down, or secure a wire (such as a sandwich bag tie) through the sleeves, you can then also use this as a loop to hang it with.

Rainhat

All you need is...

- A rubber glove
- Scissors and a pen
- Glue
- A small piece of card

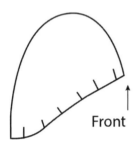

Template: Piece 1

Front →

Step 1.

Using the templates cut Piece 1 from the thumb of a latex glove including the tiny cuts around the lower edge, and cut two of the 'brim' pieces (Piece 2) from the 'body' of the glove, taking note of where the front of the hat is.

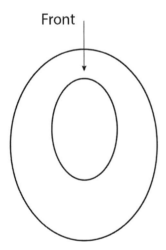

Front ↓

Template: Piece 2 (Cut 2)

Step 2.

Put a small amount of glue all the way round the outside of 'fringed' edge of the thumb piece.

Put this piece on your finger and pick up one of the two brim pieces, matching the front of the hat on the two pieces, and with the right side of the fabric uppermost, pull piece 2 down over the thumb piece until just the glued edge is left, stick this to the underside of the brim piece.

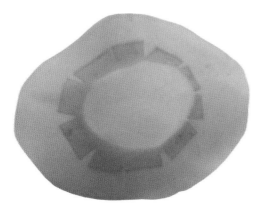

Now take the second brim piece and coat the underside completely with glue, stick this to the underside of the first brim piece 'sandwiching' the fringed edge of the thumb piece.

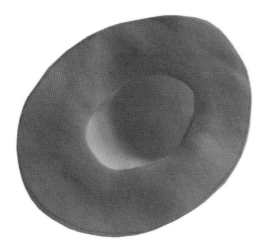

Step 3.

Cutting through both thicknesses trim the outside edge of the hat brim making sure you cut off any pen markings from drawing around the template. This also helps to seal the edge.

Finally, just fold the front of the brim up and glue to the thumb piece to hold in place. And you may need a tiny bit of filling in the top of the hat to keep the shape (scrunched up cling film is fine).

Handkerchiefs
&
Household
Linen

This chapter is aimed at showing you some ideas of projects that can be made from household linen such as old tablecloths, pillowcases, clothing, napkins, handkerchiefs, etc.

The idea is to utilise any embroidery, pictures, or prepared edges from the items. Nearly all the projects in this chapter are made from handkerchiefs, not because they are the best source of material but because I cannot guarantee that you might have the same old pillowcase or tablecloth, etc. as I have but I can be pretty sure you can get your hands on a handkerchief!

So when embarking on any of these projects please do consider any other materials that you might have stashed away that could actually be more suitable than a hanky.

Skirt

Easy:

All you need is...

- A handkerchief
- 20cm length of 4-6mm elastic
- Scissors and a pen
- Needle and thread
- Sewing machine (optional)

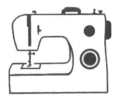

Step 1.

From your handkerchief or fabric cut a rectangle approximately 18cm x 7cm with the 'pretty' or finished edge as one of the longer sides.

On the long side of the rectangle without the finished edge turn down a hem about 1.5cm depth, it is helpful (but not essential) to iron this to give a crease.

Step 2.

Before you start sewing, lay the length of elastic under the hem (along the crease) making sure it is sticking out of both ends of the material.

Take your piece of elastic and measure in 2cm from the end, make a mark. Then measure a further 6cm from that mark and make another mark, do NOT cut the elastic at this stage.

Now sew the hem in place, being careful not to sew over the elastic. We want to end up with the elastic in a long tube. Machine sewing will give a neater finish but hand sewing is fine too.

Step 4.

Now fold the skirt in half with the right side innermost and sew up the side seam (sewing over the elastic). There is quite a lot of stress on this seam so if you're using a sewing machine it's a good idea to sew over the seam twice.

Step 3.

Pulling the elastic gently, (and not letting go of the end!) line the first mark that you made 2cm in, with the edge of the fabric – sew the elastic in place here (probably easier with a needle and thread rather than a machine).

Gently gathering the material as you go pull the other end of the elastic through the hem until the second mark is lined up with the edge of the fabric, sew the elastic in place.

Snip off the excess elastic, even up the gathering, and turn your finished skirt the right way out.

You can of course adjust the length of your skirt to suit your doll, or the occasion, the measurements here give a skirt that falls just below the knee, but you could have it shorter or go for a long evening skirt.

Why not add some braid, lace or sequins for a really special garment?

Parasols

Easy: ⭐⭐⭐⭐⭐

All you need is...

- A hanky, or fabric with a pretty edge, i.e. lace, or scalloped
- Scissors & a pen
- Needle & thread
- A cocktail stick
- A couple of beads
- Small piece of embroidery thread or very narrow ribbon
- Paint, varnish, or pen to colour the handle (if required)

These little parasols need only a very small amount of material and what we are looking for is fabric with a pretty edge, again handkerchiefs are an easy option with many having lace edges or pretty picot hems, but try looking through old clothing for pretty hems on sleeves or old pillowcases for embroidered edges, just bear in mind that as with most very small items a thinner fabric will work easier. Don't worry too much about any pattern on the fabric as this will not be very visible on the finished item.

Step 1.

The cocktail stick is going to form the handle of the parasol, so if you wish to colour it to match or contrast with your fabric do so now so that it can be drying whilst you make the next part.

If you're happy with a bare wooden handle, which can look very attractive, you can skip this step and move straight on to Step 2.

There are several different ways of colouring the handle, the simplest one being to just to colour it with a felt tip pen, you might need to go over it a few times, but it is an easy and effective option.

Almost any type of paint or wood varnish is suitable, or nail enamel is a great alternative as it's available in lots of colours and comes with a handy brush included!

I find it easiest to use something like a lump of 'tack' (or some polystyrene would do) - paint half the stick and push the dry end in into the tack, let it dry then repeat with the other end.

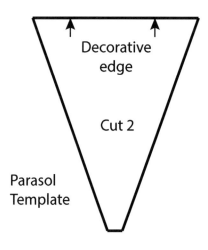

Decorative
edge

Cut 2

Parasol
Template

Step 3.

Turn this the right way out so that the seams are on the inside, you might need to use something pointed such as a knitting needle to get the point of the triangle turned out fully.

Step 2.

Copy the template above and cut 2 from your fabric matching up the 'pretty' edge.

Place the two triangles together with the right side of the fabric on the inside and sew along both the long edges using small, neat backstitch (or you can use a sewing machine if you prefer) don't sew right across the narrow end as you need to leave a tiny opening to push the cocktail stick through.

Lightly coat half the stick with glue, a tacky or quick drying glue is best. Push the glued end into the fabric cone and through the bottom. Now pinch the fabric onto the glued stick about 2cm from the top fancy edge, hold it in place and twist from the bottom end so that the fabric twists around the stick, press gently to neaten the folds of the parasol.

It is important to make sure both your hands and your work surfaces are clean before you do this as the glue will attract any dirt and your parasol could quickly end up looking a bit grubby.

Step 4.

Using your embroidery thread, or very thin ribbon if you have it, tie a bow around the parasol about 2cm down from the pretty edge, this is easier if you make a large bow, pull it tight, and then gently pull the ends through to make it smaller.

Clip off any excess thread.

Finish off by gluing a couple of beads to the top of the stick to make an attractive handle.

Sadly these are just for show and don't actually open.

Why not make one to match a special outfit?

Christening gown

All you need is...

- A hanky or fabric with a lacy corner
- A baby doll with moveable arms
- Needle and thread
- Embroidery thread or very thin ribbon
- Scissors and a pen

Please note that this project is made on the doll and fixed in place

Templates:

Hood piece

Decorative edge

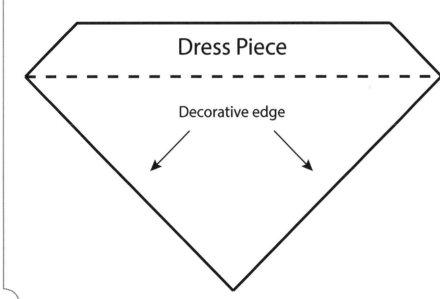

Dress Piece

Decorative edge

Step 1.

Copy the template and cut the two pieces out of the hanky or fabric that you are using. If you have quite a wide lace edge place the dotted lines of the Hood template where the lace joins the fabric and have a wider hood piece.

Fold the Hood piece in half (with the right side inside) and sew a hem in tiny backstitch as shown.

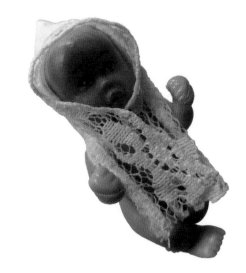

You are going to make two cuts, one each side, roughly where the dotted lines are on the template. But to get the right length of cut to fit your doll put the hood over the dolls head (without turning it the right way out) and make a tiny pen mark where the hood reaches the baby's neck - cut to this mark.

Step 3.

Take the Dress piece and fold it along the dotted line shown on the template. Beginning about 1cm in from the pointed end, start sewing a row of running stitches across to about 1cm from the other end, sewing as close as possible to the folded edge (don't fasten off).

Step 2.

Turn the Hood piece the right way out and place the hood over your dolls head, with the arms going in the side splits.

If your lace edging is very wide you might want to fold this back. If possible, just press the lace edging under your doll's chin using your fingernails.

Now gently pull the thread and gather up the stitches so that the entire length of the folded edge measures approximately 7.5cm, fasten off to hold the gather in place, and then continue sewing to bring the thread to the edge of the point (about another 1cm).

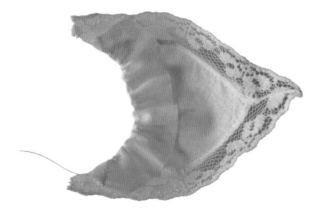

Step 5.

Put the doll's arms down again, and finish off by tying a thin ribbon or piece of embroidery thread into a bow around the dolls neck.

Step 4.

Wrap the Dress piece around the doll, by positioning the doll's arms pointing upwards and placing the back of the doll at waist height onto the centre of the gathered section, bring the point without the thread attached around the front and under the baby's arm, then wrap the other point, with the thread, across the front and sew it in place under the other arm. Cut the thread.

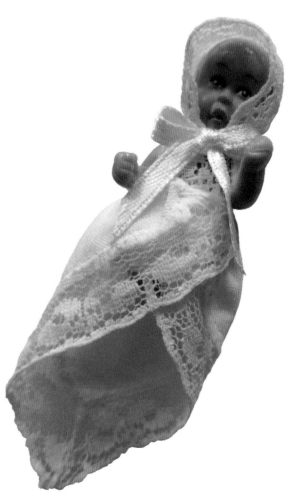

As with the parasol, it is easier to initially tie a larger bow and then gradually pull it smaller.

All that's left now is to position your baby's arms how you'd like them to be!

Embroidery set

All you need is...

- A ten pence piece, or similar
- Fabric with a tiny embroidered piece
- A small rubber band
- Tiny piece of foil (preferably gold)
- Coloured threads to match the embroidery
- Double-sided sticky tape
- Small piece of paper
- Scissors
- Glue
- Miniature scissors (optional)

Step 1.

Place the coin on the paper and draw around it. Cut it out, but cut well inside the line so that you finish with a circle slightly smaller than the coin (it doesn't have to be perfect).

Cover one side of the coin with double-sided tape, leaving a small excess as shown in the picture.   Then trim this excess to approximately 2mm all the way around.

Step 2.

Remove the backing paper and press the excess tape down onto the side of the coin. Stick the paper circle onto the coin centering carefully, this is to give a light background and also to prevent the sticky tape from staining the embroidery.

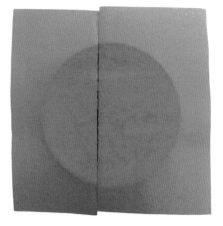

Step 3.

Take your fabric and, on the reverse side, mark and cut out a square (or circle if you prefer) with the embroidery at the centre. This will become your embroidery work so the size is up to you, but as a guide using a 10p piece I have cut a 4.5cm square

Place the fabric over the coin, with the enbroidery in the centre, and press the fabric onto the sticky tape around the edge of the coin.

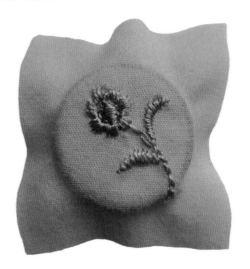

Step 4.

Apply a tiny bit of glue to the right side of the fabric all around the edge of the coin, you might find a cocktail stick useful for this. Now carefully place the rubber band around the coin onto the glue and allow to dry. If your rubber band is too big just cut it and make a neat join.

Using a little piece of foil about half the size of your smallest fingernail, make the tiniest ball you can and glue this to the rubber band to look like the screw mechanism on the hoop. If you have had to cut your rubber band to fit, place this over the join.

Step 5.

To make the bundles of cottons, loosely wrap the matching colour thread around a pen or pencil several times as shown. Slip this 'ring' of thread off the pen or pencil and squash together, finish by wrapping the thread around the middle a few times and secure with a tiny blob of glue. Snip the thread close to the centre of the 'bundle'.

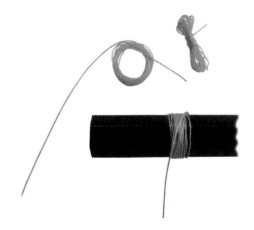

Now simply arrange your cottons, and a small pair of scissors if you have them, next to your embroidery. If you wish you can either sew or glue them in position, or leave them loose to rearrange if you prefer.

Firescreens

Moderate: ⭐⭐⭐⭐⭐

All you need is...

- A hanky. or fabric with some embroidery or a suitable pattern
- 2 Cocktail sticks
- Scissors & a pencil
- Some beads and/or jewellery findings
- Paint, or similar to colour the cocktail sticks
- Tacky glue (or PVA will do)
- Small piece of card

Step 1.

First colour your cocktail sticks, see the Parasol instructions on page 84 for ideas on how to do this, and leave them to dry whilst you prepare the next stage.

Step 2.

Ensure your hanky or fabric is well ironed.

Taking your piece of card cut 2 small rectangles (both the same size), the size can be dependant on your embroidery or fabric pattern but as a guide the rectangle used for the one shown here is 3.5cm wide and 4.5cm high. Dolls house fireplaces can also vary hugely in size so it's worth holding your rectangle in front of your fireplace just to make sure the size is compatible.

Step 3.

Place one of the rectangles on the back of your fabric positioned centrally over your design, draw around the card with a pencil. Now cut your fabric but NOT on the pencil line, leave a margin of about 1cm all around.

Step 4.

Put the rectangle back onto the reverse side of your fabric (in your pencil lines), and working on the long edges first fold the material over the card and glue in place. Once this is dry repeat on the shorter edges.

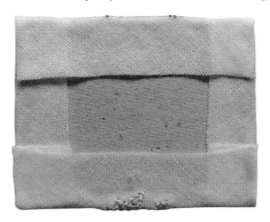

Take your second card rectangle and glue onto the back of your 'picture piece' to hide the folded edges and give a neat finish.

Step 5.

Now take your coloured cocktail sticks and add some 'feet', jewellery findings (or bead 'cups') are great for this and can be bought very cheaply but always check any broken or unused costume jewellery you may have before buying more!

If you don't have any of these a group of three small beads with another bead on top is another option, or experiment with anything you have at home.

If desired add a couple of beads to the top end of the cocktail sticks to finish them off.

Step 6.

Apply a little glue to the long edges of your rectangle and glue the cocktail sticks to the side making sure you have them level, i.e. the distance from the rectangle to the base of the foot is the same on both sides. (It's best not to try and stand it up until the glue has dried!)

Pictures

All you need is...

- Fabric with a small piece of embroidery
- A picture frame
- A piece of card
- PVA or tacky glue
- Masking tape
- Scissors & a pencil

This is a bit of a 'cheat' project as I'm afraid I can't tell you how to make a picture frame out of a hanky!

However, if you happen to have a miniature picture frame, or a suitable old brooch, a small piece of embroidery such as you might find on a hanky can make a lovely picture.

Step 1.

For a rectangular picture cover a piece of card in the same way as you would for the Firescreen, (follow steps 3 & 4 on pages 92 - 93) taking the size of your card from your frame.

The easiest way to do this is to place the frame on the card and draw inside the edge of the frame, then cut out leaving a small margin all around. Check your card fits into the frame before covering with the picture.

Don't be tempted to glue the picture in place as glue usually discolours fabrics after only a short time, so always fold the fabric over the card and glue to the back.

For a round or oval picture cut your piece of card in the same way, then place your card onto the back of your picture and lightly draw around it in pencil.

Cut the fabric leaving a 1cm margin around your pencil line, then snip the margin into tabs all around so that it looks like it has a wide fringe.

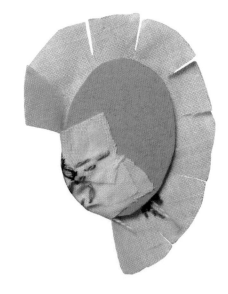

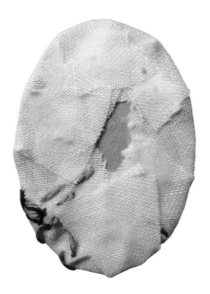

Step 2.

Insert your picture into the frame and neatly cover the back with masking tape. You might need to use a scalpel to cut the tape to fit around an oval or round frame.

Place some glue on the back of the card and one by one fold each tab over and stick down. Leave to dry.

Valance sheet

Moderate: ⭐⭐⭐⭐⭐

All you need is...

- A hanky
- Scissors and a pen
- A ruler
- Sewing machine

Step 1.

As in real life there are many different styles of beds available for your dollshouse, and different styles need different sheets.

The instructions here are for a popular style dollshouse bed that has a fixed headboard and footer and a mattress.

This design looks best with the valance only on the sides. However, unlike real beds the mattresses on model furniture are often stuck in place removing the option of tucking a sheet underneath so our sheets need to be 'made to measure' to fit snugly over the mattress.

Handkerchiefs come in all sizes, as do model beds, but generally speaking as long as your handkerchief is at least 28cm square and you position your pieces as directed you should be able to get a complete valance sheet out of one hanky. To fit 2 pillowcases as well you need a minimum of 30cm square.

First measure the top of the mattress (as a guide a double bed is around 12cm x 15cm). Now add 4cm to the width measurement and 4cm to the length as well. Cut a paper template to these measurements and place it on the hanky in the position shown, draw around it but don't cut it out just yet.

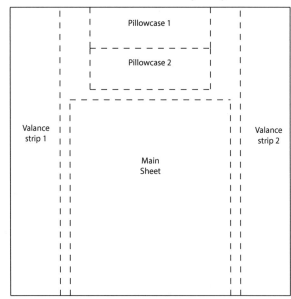

Pillowcase 1

Pillowcase 2

Valance strip 1

Valance strip 2

Main Sheet

Step 2.

Now measure the height from the floor to the top of the mattress (about 5cm). From paper, and using this measurement, cut out two strips the width of your hanky (if you aren't using a hanky you'll need them to be about 28-30cm long).

We want to use the neatly finished edge of the hanky to be the lower hem on the valance, so place these paper strip templates along two edges of your hanky either side of your main piece, as shown in the diagram.

If you are also making pillowcases out of the same hanky (see overleaf for instructions), position, and draw around the templates for these as shown on the cutting layout. Cut all your pieces out.

Step 3.

On the reverse side of the main piece of your sheet mark out a 2cm square in each corner using a pencil.

On the two sides that don't need a valance (the top and bottom) iron a small hem approx 1cm deep.

Step 4.

Make the valance sides; set your sewing machine stitch length to the longest possible, and taking one of the long strips of fabric, sew two parallel lines of stitching along the long side opposite the hemmed edge.

Holding one thread from the end of each row of stitching, gently pull to gather the fabric.

Keep gathering until your side piece fits between the two squares marked on the back of your sheet (on the long sides). Even out the gathers so that they look consistent.

Repeat with the other side piece.

Step 5.

Reduce the stitch length on your sewing machine to a more regular size. Taking one of your gathered side pieces place it on the main piece positioning it between the two marked squares. Join the two pieces together, sewing just underneath your gathering stitches. Repeat with the other side.

Step 6.

Fold the corners of your sheet as shown so that your pencil lines marking the square match up. Sew along these lines (taking in the ironed hem).

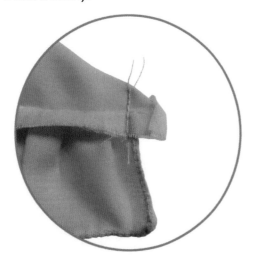

Trim off the excess fabric at the corner darts that you've just sewn and turn your sheet the right way out.

You may find the valance 'hangs' better if you lighty iron the gathers.

Position the sheet on your bed, covering the mattress, if needed use some dressmakers pins to secure the sheet in place pushing them into the mattress (if possible).

Pillows and Pillowcases

All you need is...

- A scrap of white material
- A hanky
- Small amount of filling
- Scissors, pen & ruler
- Needle & thread or a sewing machine

Pillow Step 1.

Cut a rectangle 4.5cm x 12cm from your white fabric. You might find it easier to make a paper or card template to draw around rather than measuring straight onto your fabric.

Fold the rectangle in half lengthways and sew down the two long sides using either a sewing machine or tiny backstitch.

Pillowcase Step 1.

Cut a rectangle 5cm x 14cm from your fabric, if you are using a handkerchief or similar use the 'finished' or decorative lacy edge as one of the short sides of your rectangle. If you don't have any finished edges add another 1cm to the length of your rectangle and turn a small hem on one of the short sides.

On the reverse side of your fabric fold over the opposite 'raw' short edge of the rectangle, about 1.5cm, and just crease the fold using your fingers.

Step 2.

Now turn your pillow the right way out, making sure the corners are pushed out fully giving a neat rectangle. Lightly stuff the pillow using cotton wool or some stuffing out of you own pillow, (you need such a tiny amount no one would ever notice!).

Step 3.

Sew across the open end of the pillow to finish off. When dressing your bed always make sure the 'raw' edge of the pillow goes into the pillowcase first so that it won't be seen.

Step 2.

Fold the rectangle in half lengthways, with the right side of the fabric inside, and sew down the two long sides. This time, the 'open' end will remain open (to put the pillow in) so make sure you finish off well at this edge to prevent to seam coming undone when you are using the pillowcase.

Step 3.

Insert your pillow into the pillowcase, and tuck under the folded flap just as you would with your own pillowcases.

The measurements given here are for pillows for a double bed, sometimes a single bed looks better with a slightly larger pillow, in which case just add an extra 1cm to the length of the both the pillow and the pillowcase.

Quilt & cover

Moderate: ⭐⭐⭐⭐⭐

All you need is:

- 2 Hankies, or pretty fabric
- Small piece of bubble wrap
- 6 wire sandwich bag ties
- Seed beads for buttons
- Clear tape
- Scissors and a pen
- Sewing machine
- An iron

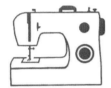

The instructions given are for a single bed, approximately 15cm x 9cm, for a double bed please use the measurements shown in brackets.

Step 1.

Cut two rectangles 15cm x 13cm (or 18cm x 13cm) from your hanky or fabric carefully locating your pattern or embroidery on one of them. If you have a large handkerchief you may get both squares out of one for the single bed.

Iron a 1cm hem along the edge that is to be the bottom of the quilt on both pieces. With right sides facing inwards place the two pieces together and sew around the other

three sides as shown. Clip the top corners off making sure you don't cut the stitching (this just makes a neater finish when you turn it the right way out).

Turn the quilt cover the right way out and iron lightly.

Step 2.

To make the quilt cut two pieces of bubble wrap 13cm x 10cm (16cm x 10cm).

Take one of the sandwich bag ties and fold over about 1cm on one end, place the folded end on the corner of one of the squares with the other end going diagonally inwards, tape in place and repeat for the other three corners.

Tape the two remaining pieces horizontally, halfway down the square.

Tape the second square on top of the piece with the wires. This is your quilt!

Step 3.

Place the quilt inside the cover pushing the folded wire tips into the corners of the cover at the top (a bit like putting on a real quilt cover!), and under the lower folded hem at the bottom corners.

Using a needle and thread fasten the bottom opening by just catching the folded edges together with a couple of stitches every 1.5cm, you can add in a seed bead here if you want it to look buttoned (if your needle is too big for your beads you can always glue them on afterwards).

Finally place your quilt on the bed and gently bend the wires inside the quilt to make it look as though it is naturally draping over the sides of the bed.

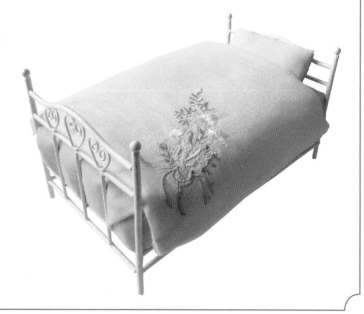

Bedspread

Moderate: ⭐⭐⭐⭐⭐

All you need is...

- Hanky or fabric with a pretty corner
- Another hanky or fabric in a contrasting colour
- Sewing machine
- Needle and thread

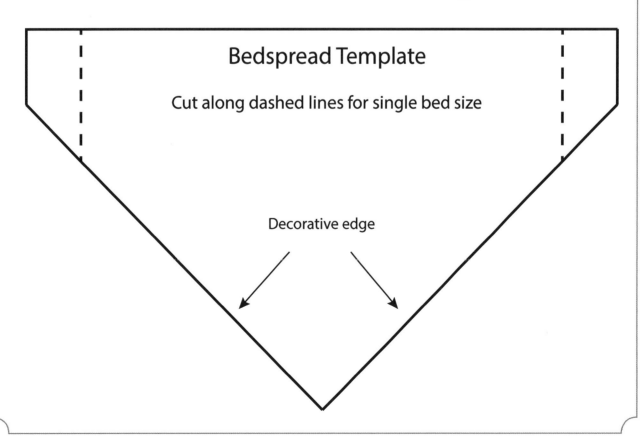

Bedspread Template

Cut along dashed lines for single bed size

Decorative edge

Step 1.

Cut 2 rectangles out of the plain fabric 14cm x 16cm for a double bed or (14cm x 13cm) for a single. (I only had a small piece of pink so I'm doing the underside of my bedspread in white, but you can have both pieces the same or experiment as you wish.)

Using the template cut out your corner piece. Position the corner piece on the rectangle that is to be the topside of your bedspread (it might be helpful to tack it in place).

Step 2.

With your fancy corner piece on the inside place the other rectangle on top and sew around the four sides but leaving a gap of approximately 5cm to be able to turn it the right way out. Snip off the corners making sure you don't cut the stitching.

Step 3.

Remove any tacking stitches and turn the bedspread the right way out, pushing gently into the corners to give a square finish. Neatly oversew the opening to finish.

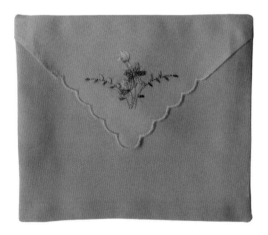

The instructions for the quilt cover and the bedspread are interchangeable, so you could use this design as the quilt cover instead.

Curtains

All you need is:

- A hanky, or fabric with a finished edge and 2 corners
- A coffee stirrer or lolly stick
- Tacky glue
- Small piece of thin ribbon or embroidery thread
- Sewing machine
- Iron

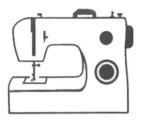

These little curtains are fixed - you can't open or close them, and when they are finished they are attached over the window simply using glue or tack.

Step 1.

The coffee stirrer or lolly stick is going to be the 'curtain rail' so cut this to the required length for your window using strong scissors or pliers.

You need to cut three strips of fabric – the top piece and two curtains. First cut out the curtains, these need to be the finished length of your required curtains by about 6cm wide, and they need to include the finished corners of your fabric (see picture overleaf).

Then cut out the top strip of fabric, this needs to be approximately twice the length of your curtain rail by about 3.5cm wide (it doesn't matter if the length is a little shorter if your hanky isn't wide enough, but don't go any longer).

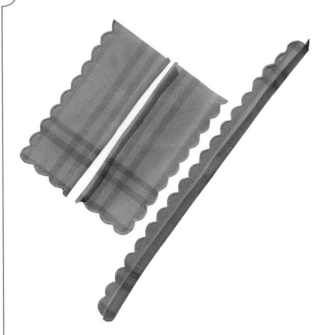

Step 4.

With the reverse side of the fabric pieces facing you tuck the curtain pieces under the ironed hem of the rail piece (just up to the fold line), one each end and pin or tack in place.

Now sew two rows of running stitch, about ½ cm apart, across the length of the rail piece catching in the two curtain pieces as you go, again don't fasten off or cut the threads.

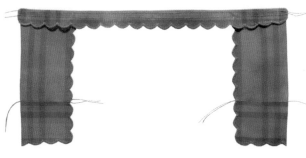

Step 2.

Take the two curtain pieces and iron a tiny hem on the long 'raw' edge. There is no need to sew this and it will look neater without the stitching.

On the long 'rail' piece iron a 1cm hem along the long raw edge.

My rail piece pictured above is simply the length of the hanky so the short sides are already finished, if yours aren't just iron a small hem as you did on the curtain pieces.

Step 3.

Sew a line of running stitch, either with a sewing machine or by hand across the width of each curtain piece about a 1/3 of the way up from the bottom, don't fasten off or cut off the threads as you will need them to gather the fabric later on.

Working on the top rail section, tie the threads together at one end to hold in place, then gently pull the two threads at the other end gathering the fabric up until it is the length of your coffee stirrer or lolly stick rail (if you have used a sewing machine you will need to separate the two threads and pull on just the top threads from each row of stitches).

Spend a few minutes evening out the gathers, particularly over the top of the two curtain strips.

Just using your fingers, make some vertical creases in the curtain strips, this will help it 'hang' more naturally when finished.

Step 5.

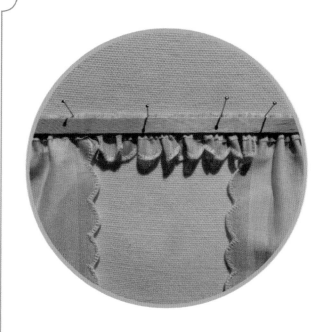

Apply a line of glue, tacky glue is best for this, along the wooden rail piece and stick it to the back of the gathered fabric lining it up with the top row of stitching. You may find it easier to pin the curtain to a cushion or pillow to hold the top edge straight whilst you stick the wooden rail in place.

Now gather up the curtain strips using the line of running stitches you did earlier (in the same way as you did for the top rail), fasten off, and finish by tying a bow around the gathered fabric.

Screen

All you need is...

- A piece of card (preferably white)
- A piece of patterned or embroidered fabric (a hanky)
- Plain or contrasting fabric (another hanky!)
- A small piece of ribbon (25cms)
- 2.5m of embroidery thread or thin cord (optional)
- Scissors & a pencil
- Tacky glue

Moderate: Moderate:

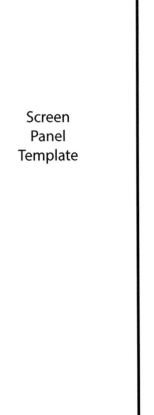

Screen
Panel
Template

Step 1.

First make sure that your fabric is very well ironed as you can't take out any creases later.

Copy and cut out the template and cut out 6 panels from your card (assuming you want to make a three-panel screen – you don't have to, choose as many panels as you like, it's your screen!).

These screens use a similar technique to that used in making the fireguards. So, on the reverse side of your fabric, place the template centrally over your embroidery or pattern and draw around it but do NOT cut on the drawn lines. Instead cut out your panel leaving a 1cm margin all around.

Repeat for the other 5 panels. You need 3 panels for the front and 3 for the back of your screen.

Step 2.

Take one of your fabric panels and place a cardboard panel inside the lines drawn on the reverse side.

Starting with the short top and bottom edges fold the hem over and glue to the cardboard. Do not put any glue on the other (front) side of the cardboard as this can sometimes stain the fabric. Next, fold and glue the two angled sides, and finally the two long sides.

We do it in this order so that a) you don't get a 'lump' of fabric folds at the top of the panel, and b) folding the long sides last gives the neatest edge to your panels.

Step 3.

The next stage is to put the thread or cord around the edges of the panels, this is a bit fiddley, and by the time you get to the sixth panel a bit tedious too, so bear in mind that this is optional, if you're happy without the extra edging it isn't necessary.

If you do want to go ahead – apply a thin coating of glue to one or two edges of the panel (I recommend putting the join at the bottom) and with the panel flat on your working surface with the right side uppermost gently press the thread onto the edge of the panel, you might find a tool such as a cocktail stick helpful here. Make sure it has stuck all the way along before progressing to the next edge. When you get to the final side simply snip the cord and glue in place.

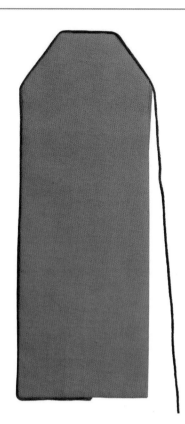

Step 4.

Once you have edged all six panels, take the three panels you plan to use for the back of the screen and lay them in a row, face down, and almost touching but not quite. Now apply some glue and stick two pieces of ribbon across all three panels as shown.

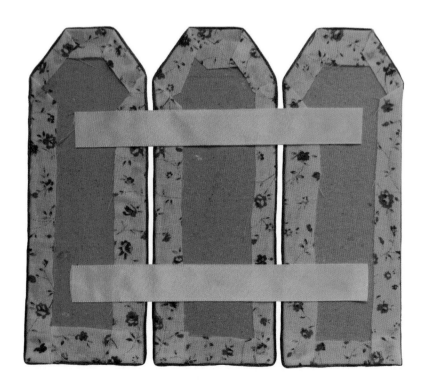

Step 5.

The final stage is to glue the front panels onto the back panels, using plenty of glue but being careful that it doesn't squeeze out of the sides attach each panel to its partner and press firmly together. For a good finish the edges needs to be firmly together all the way around, so I put mine in a bag (to stop gluing it to a surface) and put a heavy book on top until it dried thoroughly.

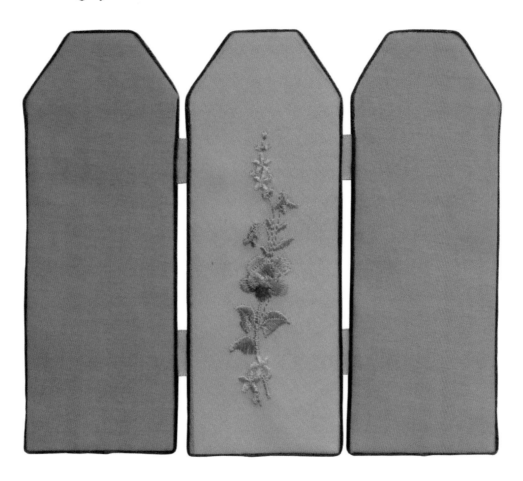

I used a completey different fabric for the back panels of my screen which gives me the option of using either side as the front view. Have fun experimenting with your own combinations, but if you choose a totally different colour for one side you will probably need to use a neutral colour edging.

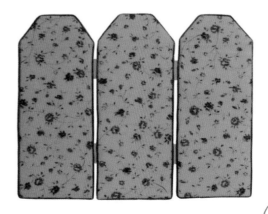

With Special Thanks to:

Yvonne Mansergh
For her valued support and enthusiasm,
and for gifting me my first dollshouse.

Nathan McGee
For his patient technical support.

Tanis Mills
For her belief and encouragement.

And to the members of Aylesbury Dollshouse Club, particularly:

Sallyanne Bartlett

Margaret Redler

Judith Halls

Jeanette Green

Diane Haylor

Karen Puddephatt

Yumi Coyte

Ann Bowles

Helen Talbot

Barbara Hastings

Sheila Rapley

Moira Balkwill

27639453R00063

Printed in Great Britain
by Amazon